UNDERSTANDING WEATHER

Humidity

by Kristin Schuetz

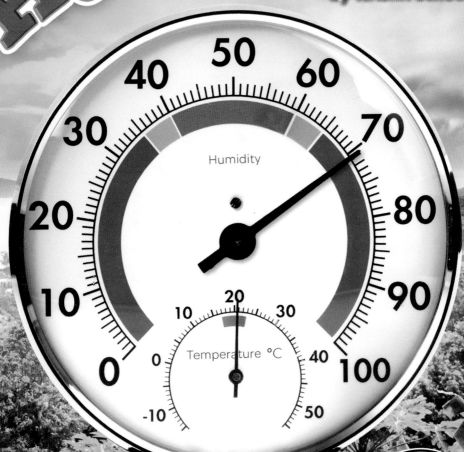

BELLWETHER MEDIA · MINNEAPOLIS, MN

Note to Librarians, Teachers, and Parents:

Blastoff! Readers are carefully developed by literacy experts and combine standards-based content with developmentally appropriate text.

Level 1 provides the most support through repetition of high-frequency words, light text, predictable sentence patterns, and strong visual support.

Level 2 offers early readers a bit more challenge through varied simple sentences, increased text load, and less repetition of high-frequency words.

Level 3 advances early-fluent readers toward fluency through increased text and concept load, less reliance on visuals, longer sentences, and more literary language.

Level 4 builds reading stamina by providing more text per page, increased use of punctuation, greater variation in sentence patterns, and increasingly challenging vocabulary.

Level 5 encourages children to move from "learning to read" to "reading to learn" by providing even more text, varied writing styles, and less familiar topics.

Whichever book is right for your reader, Blastoff! Readers are the perfect books to build confidence and encourage a love of reading that will last a lifetime!

This edition first published in 2016 by Bellwether Media, Inc.

No part of this publication may be reproduced in whole or in part without written permission of the publisher. For information regarding permission, write to Bellwether Media, Inc., Attention: Permissions Department, 5357 Penn Avenue South, Minneapolis, MN 55419.

Library of Congress Cataloging-in-Publication Data

Schuetz, Kristin, author.
  Humidity / by Kristin Schuetz.
    pages cm – (Blastoff! readers: understanding weather)
  Summary: "Relevant images match informative text in this introduction to humidity. Intended for students in kindergarten through third grade"–Provided by publisher.
  Includes bibliographical references and index.
  Audience: Ages 5-8
  Audience: K to Grade 3.
  ISBN 978-1-62617-252-4 (hardcover : alk. paper)
  1. Humidity–Juvenile literature. I. Title.
  QC915.S32 2016
  551.57′1–dc23
                          2015004211

Printed in the United States of America, North Mankato, MN.

Table of
Contents

Sometimes the air feels hot and sticky. This happens on a **humid** day.

HOT AND HUMID

SAT

HIGH
89

LOW
43

It means there is a lot of wetness in the air.

Wetness in the air is called **water vapor**.

It is water in its gas form.

Meteorologists measure water vapor to figure out humidity.

They use tools called
hygrometers.

Dew to Fog to Frost

Meteorologists also find the **dew point**. This is the **temperature** at which droplets of **dew** form.

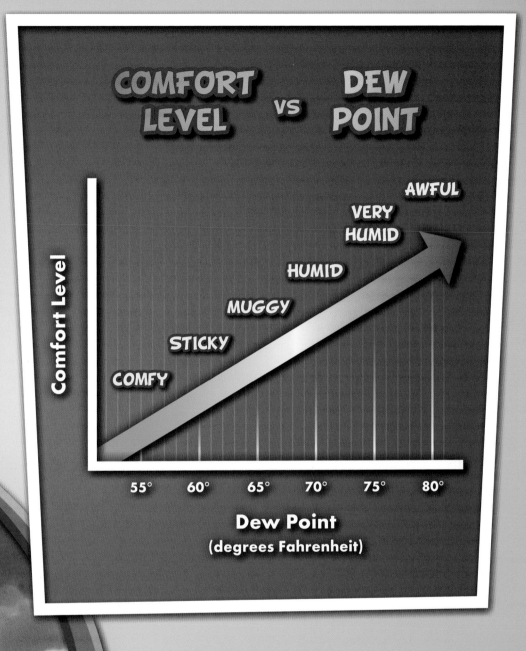

High humidity means high dew points.

Air becomes **saturated** when it is full of wetness.

Extra wetness must **condense**.
It changes from water vapor into
liquid dew.

Sometimes this extra wetness forms **fog** or **mist**. They make it hard to see.

When it is cold outside, extra wetness turns into **frost**.

15

High and Low Humidity

Tropical rain forests are among the most humid places.

Deserts are known for being
the opposite of humid. They
are very dry.

High and low humidity affect us in different ways.

High humidity makes our bodies sweaty and hair frizzy.

Low humidity makes temperatures feel colder than they really are.

Our skin becomes dry and
cracked. Lotion and lip balm
are a must!

Glossary

condense—to change from a gas into a liquid

dew—water droplets that appear on surfaces when the air is saturated

dew point—the temperature at which conditions are right for dew to form

fog—small water droplets floating in the air near the ground

frost—a thin layer of ice crystals

humid—having a lot of water vapor in the air

hygrometers—tools used to measure the humidity in the air

meteorologists—people who study and predict the weather

mist—small water droplets floating in the air or falling as light rain

saturated—filled to the point of having no more room

temperature—how hot or cold it is outside

tropical rain forests—warm, wet forests that get a lot of rain

water vapor—water in the form of a gas

To Learn More

AT THE LIBRARY
Hammersmith, Craig. *The Water Cycle.* Mankato, Minn.: Capstone Press, 2012.

Rabe, Tish. *Oh Say Can You Say What's the Weather Today? All About Weather.* New York, N.Y.: Random House, 2004.

Rattini, Kristin Baird. *Weather.* Washington, D.C.: National Geographic Society, 2013.

ON THE WEB
Learning more about humidity is as easy as 1, 2, 3.

1. Go to www.factsurfer.com.

2. Enter "humidity" into the search box.

3. Click the "Surf" button and you will see a list of related web sites.

With factsurfer.com, finding more information is just a click away.

Index

The images in this book are reproduced through the courtesy of: manfredxy, front cover, p. 9; Iakov Kalinin, front cover; solarseven, weather symbols (front cover, all interior pages); Jorg Hackemann, pp. 4-5; Creative Travel Projects, pp. 6-7; Dreamstimepoint, pp. 8-9; Patrick Pleul/ AP Images, pp. 10-11; artshock, pp. 12-13; bikeriderlondon, pp. 14-15; psv, p. 15; Egon Zitter, p. 16; LucynaKoch, p. 17; Bloomimage/ Corbis, p. 18; lr1972, p. 19; cliplab, p. 20; JPC-Prod, p. 21.